WE BEAT THE STREET

by
Drs. Sampson Davis, George Jenkins, and Rameck Hunt
with Sharon M. Draper

Teacher Guide

Written by
Jackie Crnkovich

Note

The 2006 Puffin Books paperback edition of the book, © 2005 by The Three Doctors LLC, was used to prepare this guide. Page references may differ in other editions. ISBN 0-14-240627-9

Please note: This book deals with sensitive, mature issues. Parts contain references to substance abuse and violence. Please assess the appropriateness of this book for the age level and maturity of your students prior to reading and discussing it with them.

ISBN 978-1-56137-562-2

To order, contact your local school supply store, or—
Novel Units, Inc.
P.O. Box 97
Bulverde, TX 78163-0097

Web site: novelunits.com

Table of Contents

Skills and Strategies

Thinking
   Analysis, compare/contrast,
   research, critical thinking,
   evaluation, interpretation

Comprehension
   Cause/effect, prediction,
   inference

Vocabulary
   Target words, definitions,
   application

Listening/Speaking
   Discussion, report, debate,
   interview

Writing
   Essay, prose, letter, poetry

Literary Elements
   Point of view, characterization,
   setting, theme, genre

Across the Curriculum
   Art—painting;
   Music—songwriting;
   Social Studies—current events

Genre: nonfiction; memoir

Setting: New Jersey, primarily inner-city Newark

Point of View: third person with first-person commentaries at the end of each chapter

Themes: peer pressure—positive and negative; setting goals; friendship; perseverance through adversity; the power of dreams

Style: narrative with direct commentary at the end of each chapter

Tone: serious, didactic, inspirational

Conflict: person vs. person; person vs. self; person vs. society

Date of First Publication: 2005

Summary

"The Three Doctors," as the authors have come to be known, first meet and become friends in high school in Newark, New Jersey during the 1980s. All three are intelligent boys, but growing up in the inner city seems to limit their life options. Further, street life poses temptations to the boys and threatens to swallow them up as it has so many other young people. By chance, they find themselves at a presentation about a Seton Hall University program for promising minority students. The boys decide to seize this opportunity; they form a pact to help one another journey through the program. This is a story of friendship and perseverance as the young men set out to pursue a dream that once seemed impossible.

About the Authors

The Three Doctors grew up in Newark, New Jersey and attended University High, a school for high-performing students. It was there that they met and formed their pact to go through the Seton Hall Pre-Medical/Pre-Dental Plus Program. Dr. George Jenkins went on to graduate from the University of Medicine and Dentistry of New Jersey and to practice and teach dentistry. Drs. Sampson Davis and Rameck Hunt graduated from the Robert Wood Johnson Medical School. Dr. Davis became an emergency-medicine physician, while Dr. Hunt pursued a career in internal medicine. The Three Doctors maintained their friendship throughout and went on to create The Three Doctors Foundation. Their foundation helps inner-city youth through education and mentoring. They have written two other books describing their experiences: *The Pact*, their story for older audiences, and *The Bond*, which details their relationships with their fathers.

Sharon M. Draper is a professional educator and author with numerous awards and honors to her name. She received the National Teacher of the Year award in 1997, is a winner of several Coretta Scott King awards, and is a *New York Times* bestselling author. She has taught English at the junior high and high school levels for over 30 years. In addition, she has served on many boards that promote effective teaching practices. Her novels, written for young adults, include the highly acclaimed *Tears of a Tiger, Forged by Fire, Darkness Before Dawn, Romiette and Julio, Double Dutch, Copper Sun,* and *November Blues*. Mrs. Draper lives with her husband in Cincinnati, Ohio.

Characters

Sampson Davis: one of the three doctors; lives with his mother and siblings; is smart, determined, and tough; pursues a career in emergency medicine

George Jenkins: perhaps the most serious and focused of the three doctors; becomes interested in dentistry at age 11 after a visit to the dentist; chooses a career in dentistry over medicine

Rameck Hunt: high-spirited and the most inclined to trouble among the three doctors; loves acting and the limelight; lives with his drug-addicted mother and has a close relationship with his grandmother, "Ma"; goes on to practice internal medicine

Ruthener Davis: "Moms"; Sampson's tough but loving mother; tries to keep her kids out of trouble

Andre Davis: Sampson's older brother

Ma: Rameck's loving grandmother who maintains high expectations for Rameck's future

Rameck's mother: hardworking woman who struggles with a drug addiction

Garland: George's older, less mature brother

Miss Viola Johnson: George's beloved third-grade teacher; works tirelessly to expose her students to life outside of the inner city; pushes students to dream big

Noody and Will: Sampson's neighborhood friends

The Bomb: an infamous drug dealer in Sampson's neighborhood; beats a man with a baseball bat

Jack: owner of the corner grocery store; tries to terrify kids caught stealing

Dr. Thomas: George's dentist; answers all of George's questions about dentistry

Reggie: security guard at the cemetery who gives kung fu lessons; talks to Sampson about setting goals and relying on inner strength

Eddie: older kid in the neighborhood; tricks Sampson into stealing carpet-cleaning equipment for him

Razor Sizemore: Sampson's 12-year-old friend; dies in a fatal car accident while running drugs

Hock, Spud, and Buddy: Sampson's friends from the streets

Carla Dickson: student development specialist in the Seton Hall program; mentors the three doctors through college and medical/dental school

© Novel Units, Inc.

Background Information

The following information will enhance students' understanding of the book.

The Three Doctors have written this book expressly for a young audience. They present their story as a lesson in friendship, positive peer pressure, overcoming obstacles, and pursuing dreams against those obstacles. They grew up in Newark, the largest city in New Jersey, located just five miles from Manhattan, New York. Once a prosperous industrial city, Newark went through a long period of decline following World War II. The city reached its nadir as the three doctors were growing up during the 1970s and 1980s. Most of its middle-class population moved away, leaving behind poverty and urban blight. Newark is currently undergoing a slow renaissance, with a number of civic building projects revitalizing the downtown area.

Seton Hall University is a Catholic university located in South Orange, New Jersey. It still offers the Pre-Medical/Pre-Dental Plus Program the three doctors went through in its fledgling years. Its goal is to steer promising underprivileged students through college and medical school.

The Three Doctors have two Web sites where students can read further about their work and even engage in conversation with the doctors. The sites can provide added inspiration for readers of the book. The sites are: www.threedoctorsfoundation.org and www.threedoctors.com (active at time of publication).

Initiating Activities

Use one or more of the following to introduce the book.

1. Have each student make a list of five to ten goals or dreams s/he has. Next to each goal, the student should indicate how attainable it seems on a scale of one to five, one being completely unattainable and five being completely attainable. Save this list to look at again after reading the book.

2. Have students write a descriptive essay about the neighborhood in which they live. Include descriptions of the homes and businesses, as well as the kinds of people who live and work there. Do the residents of the neighborhood interact with one another? How well do they know each other? What do residents expect of the young people who grow up there?

3. Ask the students to respond in writing to this statement: "All Americans have the same opportunities to achieve." Allow volunteers to share their responses and brainstorm a list of challenges young adults face growing up in America's inner cities. Depending on your students, this list will be generated from either personal experiences or from information they have heard or read. Discuss the generated list as a class.

4. Read the introduction together in class. Talk about how, although told in story form, the events recounted in the book are true. Ask students if the introduction compels them to read the book. What expectation(s) do they have about the book?

5. Have students begin a Prediction Chart (see page 20 of this guide) to use as they read the book.

Introduction–Chapter Four

In the book, chapters switch between The Three Doctors, telling each of their stories. In the beginning, they are presented as young children. Sampson at age eight is a tough, determined kid trying to keep up with his older brother. He smashes his foot in the opening chapter and goes to the hospital. Young Rameck is sent to the principal's office in the Catholic school he attends. He is a smart, high-spirited, impulsive kid who is no stranger to trouble. His mother and his grandmother, Ma, attempt to instill good values early on. George is a serious kid and interested student who eats up everything his wonderful third-grade teacher, Miss Johnson, has to offer. Sampson faces violence in the midst of a pick-up baseball game. Later, Sampson and his friends make a ludicrous attempt to steal Icees.

Vocabulary
apathy
retrospect
daunting
swaggered
hoisted
intensify
loomed
mused
sparse
debris
asserted

Discussion Questions

1. Based on this first section, what is your impression of Newark and the projects? *(The surroundings are tough, and the kids need to look and act tough to survive. The streets and parks are strewn with trash, and the apartment buildings are in disrepair—no lighting in the halls, broken elevators, etc. Drug dealers are rampant, as portrayed in the incident involving the baseball bat. Crime is so common that the boys see stealing Icees as nothing more than a failed attempt at cooling down. None of the boys indicate the presence of a father. College does not seem to be in anyone's plans.)*

2. Describe Sampson's experience at the hospital. What do you learn about him based on his reactions? *(He is fascinated by what he sees. The x-ray machine is like "magic," and he says he could have looked at the films for hours. Not only does Sampson demonstrate a natural attraction to a medical setting, he shows himself to be a bright and curious child. All his potential is apparent.)*

3. How well does the principal at Rameck's school seem to understand him? What feelings does she bring out in Rameck? *(Rameck articulates why he thinks he gets into trouble, but the principal doesn't make much of an attempt to understand him. Rameck indicates his schoolwork is too easy and that he finishes it quickly and then gets bored. She focuses only on his lack of self-control and doesn't acknowledge his academic achievements. By recommending him for special education, she proves that she is not considering his potential and views him only as a troublemaker. This attitude leaves Rameck feeling "angry and stupid.")*

4. Give your assessment of Rameck's family from Chapter Two. *(He describes his mother as beautiful and hardworking, but there are indications that something is wrong. His grandmother assures Rameck of his mother's love but says "…sometimes life gets bigger than she is…" [p. 18]. His grandmother, Ma, is warm and loving. She and his mother clearly have high expectations for Rameck, expectations he fears he won't live up to.)*

5. What positive messages does George's third-grade teacher convey to her students? *(Poor black kids can study Shakespeare—even in third grade—and appreciate it. They can enjoy the arts and attend a concert and be expected to behave. It is acceptable to be smart and to achieve. College is attainable.)*

6. To which of The Three Doctors as children can you most relate? Which would most likely have been your friend at that age? *(Answers will vary. Sampson comes across as determined, tough, and smart. Rameck is smart and spirited but lacks self-control. George is quiet, serious, intelligent, and hardworking.)*

© Novel Units, Inc.

7. Discuss Sampson and his friends' attitudes when they set out to steal the Icees. How do their actions reflect both their ages and their circumstances? *(The chapter begins with an act of violence and drug dealing. The children live in a place where crime is rampant, so pilfering snacks for which they have no money doesn't feel like much of a crime in comparison. Their "plan" is comical in its stupidity. The boys have no sense of how obvious their actions are—sticking Icees down their shorts. As is typical of children, they never consider what will happen if they are caught.)*

Supplementary Activities

1. Miss Johnson plays an important role in developing George's love of learning and instills in him a sense of possibility. Write an essay about a special teacher you have had, describing his or her personality as well as the effect s/he has had on you.

2. Using the Character Chart on page 21 of this guide, keep a list of events that happen as you read about each of the three boys.

3. Self-control is an ongoing challenge for Rameck from an early age. Write a narrative about a time you failed to exhibit self-control. Describe in detail the situation, including your feelings at the time and the consequences.

Chapters Five–Nine

The boys grow older and begin facing the challenges and dangers of the inner city. Ma gives Rameck money for acting lessons. He ends up giving it to his mother, who apparently uses the cash to buy drugs rather than paying the overdue electric bill. Later, he and his friends find themselves in a gunfight with another neighborhood's gang. Sampson starts taking kung fu lessons with a neighborhood mentor, Reggie, who encourages Sampson and his friends to focus on the positive. This contrasts with Sampson getting tricked into a shoplifting scheme and then seeing a 12-year-old friend die while driving a car on a drug run. George goes to the dentist to get fitted for his braces and is entranced by the experience. He and Sampson take the test to enter University High School in the seventh grade; Rameck comes to the school in ninth grade and lands the part of Scrooge in *A Christmas Carol*.

Vocabulary
plaintively
lanky
gait
inquisitive
sinews
warily
deterrent
regally
sauntered
lumbered

Discussion Questions

1. Much of Chapter Five centers around the difficult financial decisions Rameck's family must make. Discuss some of these decisions and what they mean to family members. Reflect on how their situation compares to your family's. *(Ma would like to be able to give Rameck everything he wants, but she really has to consider the value of commodities. For example, she won't give Rameck $50 for shoes, but she is willing to sacrifice her rent money if it means he can pursue a dream. If Rameck were willing to sell drugs, he could have all the money he wants, but he refuses to get involved. His mother's drug addiction has made her financially irresponsible. It's heartbreaking to see her waste Ma's and Rameck's sacrifices. Answers will vary.)*

2. Discuss Rameck's decision to give Ma's cash to his mother. In your opinion, did he do the right thing? Why or why not? *(Answers will vary. In support: He had his baby sister and her needs to consider. Given their situation, a portfolio of photos for a long shot at an acting career might seem too trivial. As an adult reflecting back, Rameck does not regret giving his mother the money, although he would have been more careful about how he did it. Against: He should have suspected his mother would be irresponsible; obviously other poor choices had gotten the family to this point.)*

3. George states, "…I knew the moment I walked into that [dental] office that I had found what I wanted to do for the rest of my life" (p. 49). How might the dentist himself have contributed to the formulation of George's dream? *(Like the doctor who had looked at Sampson's foot years earlier, the dentist noted George's curiosity and fed it. He took time to answer questions and explain things. Had he simply done his job, George's experience would have been one of indifference. The doctor illustrates the value of mentors who take an interest in children's futures.)*

4. Chapter Seven contains three clear parts: kung fu lessons with Reggie, the shoplifting incident, and Razor's car crash and death. Why do the authors choose these three events to capture Sampson's life at age 11? How do the events relate to one another? *(Through kung fu, Reggie presents a positive alternative to life on the streets. He tries to teach the boys about setting goals and building inner strength. The two stories that follow show the temptations the boys constantly face, illustrating how difficult Reggie's advice is to put into practice. When Sampson is arrested, his friends think it is "cool." He has finally earned his stripes. Being arrested is an expected rite of passage. Razor began the karate classes with Sampson but dropped out to deal drugs. Like Sampson, Razor found that "getting in trouble was so much easier than pretending to be an ocean" [p. 53]. Temptations continually thwart the boys' desires to make more of themselves.)*

5. Discuss reasons why students in the book would rather be perceived as dumb or as slackers than achievers. How does this attitude compare to the culture in your school? *(In the schools characterized in the book, it's cooler to fail in school than to excel. It's better to be considered a cheater than to be thought of as smart. When the cards are stacked against you, it's less risky to embrace failure than to aspire towards something greater. Answers will vary.)*

6. Why does Rameck stay in contact with his old friends after he starts at University High School? Can you relate to his desire to maintain these ties, despite obvious negative consequences? *(In a neighborhood of broken families, Rameck's included, kids form strong bonds with their friends. The desire to fit in and be "cool" is very strong for all teenagers. Furthermore, there's a certain rush in facing the dangerous situations in which the boys get involved. When one is surrounded by so much negative peer pressure, it's hard to see a better path. Answers will vary.)*

Supplementary Activities

1. Dr. Hunt (Rameck) writes, "In life you are going to have to make some hard decisions. Always try and make sure you make them with the very best intentions" (p. 43). Write about a time you had a difficult decision to make. Was there a right and wrong decision? Explain the choice you made and the thought processes that went into your choice. How do you feel about that decision now?

2. George's trip to the dentist leaves him with a dream of what he'd like to be when he grows up. Is there something you dream of doing or becoming? Write an essay about that dream. Try to recall how it originated, and describe the people who have nurtured or inspired your dream. Research how you might attain your dream, and include the information in your essay.

3. Think about a short- or long-term goal you have. Identify and list all the obstacles that potentially lie along the path to that goal. In a paragraph, compare your obstacles to those faced by the three doctors growing up in Newark's projects. Discuss your list with the class.

4. Write a narrative about a time you gave in to peer pressure despite knowing it was wrong. Or conversely, write about a time you stood up against negative peer pressure. Tell the event as a story, incorporating vivid description and dialogue.

5. Add new observations to your Character Chart.

Chapters Ten–Thirteen

In tenth grade, Rameck becomes friends with Sampson and George, and they begin to support and encourage one another. They continue, however, to face a number of temptations. Sampson comes close to selling drugs but backs out at the last moment. Rameck is almost expelled from school for spraying Silly String in a teacher's face. Later, he gets into even greater trouble when he participates in the beating of a crack addict. Rameck stabs the addict in the leg and ends up in jail. On a more positive note, he leads the student body on a successful protest for cultural diversity in the curriculum. Also, the three boys happen upon a presentation by Seton Hall University, inspiring them to make the pact that is central to their story.

Vocabulary
malignant
seethed
insubordinate
entrepreneur
incredulously
conviction
blustery
cowering
bravado
bristled

Discussion Questions

1. When Sampson walks away from Spud and the drugs, the narrator says, "he'd been able to navigate that delicate road between what was right and what was real" (p. 80). Normally we describe a choice of that nature as being between right and wrong. Why use the word "real" rather than "wrong"? *(In Chapter Ten, Sampson has had a gun pulled on him and has been offered drugs to take and drugs to sell. The vices in the neighborhood are so pervasive they are no longer viewed as an objective wrong, they are a way of life.)*

2. When Sampson turns down drugs on his birthday, Hock accuses him of thinking he's better than his friends. Relate this incident to Sampson's conversation with Rameck and George earlier in Chapter Ten. Why is staying clean such a challenge in their surroundings? *(Negative peer pressure surrounds the three friends. They live in an environment where trying hard in school and working to achieve are not the norm. They fear that by not going along, they'll appear "stupid or scared or weak" [p. 75]. Often it is "just easier to go along than to say something" [p. 75]. Sampson also acknowledges a certain rush from getting away with doing something wrong. All this speaks to the power of peer pressure. Without the positive peer pressure they're providing one another, they would probably fall prey to the streets.)*

3. Discuss the walkout Rameck and the other U.S.O. members stage. Were you surprised by their success? What did Rameck gain from this experience? *(The U.S.O. members organize a peaceful walk to the Board of Education headquarters in the name of cultural diversity in curriculum and better school conditions. The superintendent grants some of their demands, and they prove their ability to take positive action without resorting to violence. Answers will vary. Rameck experiences pride and a sense of accomplishment, both feelings not readily experienced in his environment.)*

4. As the boys discuss their futures, what obstacles to their success become apparent? Compare these obstacles to those you face in achieving your goals. *(Money is one of the biggest problems. It's required to go to college or to start a business. They also have very little knowledge of what help is available to them. They have no knowledge, for example, of scholarships or work-study programs. They are given little or no direction and are unaware of opportunities. Answers will vary.)*

5. The narrator describes the incident with the crack addict on the playground and includes a broad range of emotions the boys feel. Make a list of all the emotions the boys experience before, during, and after the beating and stabbing of the man. Discuss the relationship between violence and emotion in this incident and in general. What allows people to check their emotions? *(Emotions: boredom, disgust, protectiveness, anger, rage, fear, surprise; The prevalence of all these emotions throughout the episode illustrates how the boys abandon any thought or self-control and instead act purely on feeling. Rameck tells his mother, "We didn't mean to hurt him. We just got carried away!" [p. 105]. Students should discuss the role self-control plays in a person's ability to act wisely. People need to feel, but they also need to understand how to control their feelings.)*

6. What lessons does Rameck learn during his time in jail? What are his most enduring realizations? *(He realizes all the horror stories about jail are true. He also realizes what it means to lose one's freedom. In jail, the ability to make choices is nonexistent. He also recognizes the tragedy of the inmates who have given up, are resigned to time in a jail, and have no goals or options. These realizations strengthen Rameck's resolve to make better decisions.)*

Supplementary Activities

1. When Rameck addresses the reader about his time in jail he says, "I had given up on my chance to make choices and freely decide what I wanted to do each day. It was stifling" (p. 108). Make a list of all the choices you make throughout a day. Draw a single line through any choice that wouldn't be available to you in jail.

2. The Silly String episode almost brought disastrous consequences upon Rameck. Discuss the types of choices that could lead to school expulsion or worse. Have a class debate over the fairness of these consequences. If you disagree with their fairness, state why and give a more reasonable consequence for a particular action.

3. Continue adding to your Character Chart.

Chapters Fourteen–Seventeen

As the boys near the end of high school, Sampson is arrested for armed robbery and, as a juvenile, gets a probationary sentence. The boys apply and are accepted to the Pre-Medical/ Pre-Dental Plus Program at Seton Hall University, attending a special summer program to get them ready for the rigors of college. Rameck finds himself in trouble once again for attacking a fellow resident at the dorm, but he avoids expulsion when the boy's mother declines pressing charges. The three young men begin an organization, *Ujima*, which aims to reach out to kids in the inner city.

Vocabulary
exulted
unfazed
loping
admonished
brash
remediation
affirmation
pulmonary
antagonize
dissipated

Discussion Questions

1. Sampson steals partly to have nice things like the kids who deal drugs. Talk about this temptation. Can you relate? Do you ever see yourself or your peers acting out of a desire to have more or at least as much as those around you? How do you overcome this desire? *(Sampson is frustrated that for all his hard work, he has fewer material possessions than those who work half as hard and not as honestly as he does. Answers will vary.)*

2. Rameck's and Sampson's stories of jail time are very similar. Compare the two experiences: the temptations that led them there, the justifications they make, and their feelings during and after the crimes. *(Both feel tied to their neighborhood friends and fail to achieve the total focus on goals that George seems to have. Both groups of neighborhood friends are aimless and looking for ways to fill empty hours. Rameck's crime is unplanned, but the boys at first feel that the beating is justified because the victim is an addict. Sampson's actions are planned, and he feels they are justified by the fact that his crew is just stealing from dealers. Both boys get in bigger trouble because of the presence of weapons. Both express shame in the face of their families' reactions. Both events are turning points in the boys' lives. They are able to assess the negative turn their lives are taking and recommit themselves to the goal of attending college.)*

3. Despite the serious trouble Rameck and Sampson get into, they maintain an advantage over their friends. What enables them to look critically at their actions and turn things around while their friends continue to spiral downward? *(The support of their families is evident, seen especially in Sampson's mother's plea for him at court. Also, they are smart, and by having the opportunity to attend a better high school, their eyes are opened to greater opportunities. While they consider college, their friends scoff at it. Even though they repeatedly get pulled back into street life, they maintain an awareness of a brighter future.)*

4. Discuss how the pact affects the interview results for the boys. How might the outcome have been different without the pact? *(The pact gives them the confidence to pursue Seton Hall. They come to use one another "as crutches when one felt weak, as tools when another needed information, and as weapons to face the future together as they headed into the unknown" [p. 122]. Carla Dickson seems to take great interest in the pact, and it influences her decision to accept all three young men, knowing they will come with a built-in support system. Without the positive peer pressure the pact provides, it is likely that any one of them would have given up or succumbed to the temptations they confronted daily.)*

5. How do the three young men respond to the high expectations placed on them in the program? What role do you see the expectations of others—either positive or negative—playing in your own education? Do you feel the expectations placed on you are what they should be? *(The boys rise to the expectations placed on them. Rameck is told he can do better, so he does. Sampson is told not to miss an assignment, and he "accepted the challenge and never missed one" [p. 130]. They all thrive under the belief of others that they can achieve their goals. George gives an inspired speech even though he is the shyest of the three. Answers will vary.)*

6. What sorts of adjustments do the three young men make in their new lives? Why, with all that Seton Hall offers them, might Rameck feel "restless and incomplete"? *(The boys have never lived as minorities among whites before. Previously, their world was very self-contained, and when they did venture outside their neighborhood, they were often regarded with fear or suspicion. Sampson says, "It's just hard to get used to feeling normal around here" [p. 138]. We see in Rameck's attack on a fellow dorm resident that he hasn't learned to let his guard down. He goes on the offensive because it's what he knows. While the change is all seemingly positive, it's not surprising that it leaves Rameck and possibly the others feeling confused. As comfortable as Seton Hall is, they can't abandon their pasts without abandoning themselves.)*

7. Why do people keep giving Rameck second chances? Could you have done the same if you were the mother of the boy Rameck attacked? *(Rameck is fortunate that he encounters people throughout his life who seem to want him to succeed in spite of the odds against him. There must be a quality in him people respond to that makes them want to champion his cause. Answers will vary, but discussion can be steered toward forgiveness, mistakes and second chances, and even "zero tolerance" policies in schools.)*

Supplementary Activities

1. Make a mini-pact with a couple of your friends with a short-term goal in mind. For example, decide to work for a good grade on a test or to help one another avoid junk food for a day. Write a journal entry about the experience. If you succeeded, how did working with a group help? If you failed to meet your goal as a group, what factors contributed to the failure?

2. Who in your life has the greatest expectations for you? Write an essay about your relationship with that person and what their expectations mean to you.

3. Have a class debate to address the following statement: Dressing professionally positively influences a person's relationship with his or her client. Prepare an opening argument, and plan points of rebuttal for the opposite side.

4. Continue adding to your Character Chart.

5. Select one character from the book to analyze. Complete the Characterization chart on page 22 of this guide.

Chapters 18–Conclusion

George and Rameck start to pursue a rap music career and think about giving up medical school, but finances return them to their original goal. The three young men finish college and begin medical and dental school; they become separated for the first time in years. They struggle to adapt themselves to new worlds, but all three persevere and graduate. Sampson, the one who struggles the most with medical school, initially lands a residency in a medical field that is unexciting to him. With further effort and a stroke of luck, he ends up working in the Newark hospital in which he was born. The boys' story ends with lessons-learned advice from the three doctors to their young readers.

Vocabulary
tumultuous
acclimated
livid
genially
limbo
palatable

Discussion Questions

1. Do you think the boys should have abandoned their pursuit of a rap career for less flashy but more stable medical careers? Did they owe it to anyone to stick to their original plan? *(Answers will vary. One might argue that Rameck has had a passion for the stage since a young age, and he might have enjoyed a performing career more than medicine. On the other hand, they worked hard to get into the program. Their families and others, like Carla Dickson, sacrificed to help these young men. They took spots in a program that other minority students could have had, and it might seem unfair to throw that away for an uncertain career in entertainment.)*

2. Although academics don't seem to pose great problems for the three doctors, Chapter Nineteen illustrates some of the challenges their schooling creates. Discuss some of the difficulties the young men and their families face throughout their education. *(Although the boys are on scholarships, their families still face additional costs plus lack of income while the boys are in school. George talks about his mother working 14-hour days to help him. They also have trouble adapting to a new environment where they are minorities. They often feel alone and out of place. George's inability to knot a tie illustrates the disadvantaged positions in which the young men often find themselves.)*

3. Discuss Rameck's final brush with the police. Note the variety of emotions he feels throughout. How does this scrape differ from others Rameck has been in with the law? What does it illustrate about the injustices the men face despite their accomplishments? *(Unlike the other times Rameck gets into trouble, this time he is completely innocent. He reports feeling embarrassed, angry, and afraid. He has no control over this event, and it could derail all of his plans. "Driving While Black" [p. 162] constitutes racial prejudice against minorities and is another example of the challenges these young men face.)*

4. Discuss the improbability of Sampson ending up in his desired specialty at his home hospital. How does this one experience illustrate any number of the themes and lessons of the three doctors' stories? *(The way in which Sampson lands this job underscores the theme that with hard work and determination any dream can become possible, even for poor kids in the inner city. It's also an example of turning failure into success. Had he initially matched in emergency medicine, he likely never would have learned of the opening in Newark. And, instead of giving up, Sampson tried again and landed his dream job. Faith, hard work, and determination all come into play.)*

Supplementary Activities

1. We're told the meaning of "*Ujima*," one of the seven principles of Kwanzaa. Research the names and meanings of the other six principles. Choose one of the six, and as a class discuss how the doctors live their lives to reflect that principle.

2. Sampson relates feeling very out of sorts in medical school. He has a lot of trouble adjusting to what seems to be a foreign environment. Write a narrative about a time you felt out of place. Describe what about the situation made you feel out of place and how you responded.

3. Complete your Character Chart. Go back and circle words that appear multiple times. For each of the three doctors, choose three adjectives you feel best sum up his character.

4. Examine the dialogue between Sampson and Jacquie Johnson, the resident coordinator for Newark Beth Israel Hospital, with the Using Dialogue chart on page 23 of this guide.

5. Use the Effects of Reading chart on page 24 of this guide to record your reactions to the book.

Post-reading Discussion Questions

1. Although autobiographical, the authors write their story principally in third person and in narrative, nonfiction style. What is the effect on the reader? Also, what is the purpose of the "conversations" with the doctors following each chapter? *(By employing storytelling techniques often associated with fiction, they engage the readers and make the events of their lives more compelling. The dialogue probably didn't occur exactly as presented, but it is effective in bringing the story to life. Events may also have been altered or condensed to tell the tale, although the essential truth remains. The follow-up conversations allow readers to hear the voice of each doctor directly. They are effective in conveying the lesson presented in each chapter. The doctors wrote the book not just because they have a good story to tell but to change the lives of their readers for the better. Their writing techniques ensure that readers receive the messages they mean to convey.)*

2. Discuss the role of positive and negative peer pressure in the lives of Rameck, Sampson, and George. Cite examples of each. How well do you think the boys fare against negative peer pressure? After reading the book, has your own outlook on peer pressure changed at all? Explain. *(They all manage to stay away from using or selling drugs, a huge part of their culture. A good example of this is Sampson's refusal to do drugs with his friends on his birthday. Their records are not perfect, however, and they do make mistakes. Sampson takes part in the drugdealer hold-ups; Rameck beats and stabs a crack addict. On the other hand, the boys resist the pressure to do badly in school. The best example of positive peer pressure is the pact. With each other's support, they overcome all of the negative influences. Answers will vary. Given where the young men end up and the negative influences in their lives, it is reasonable to say that they fare very well against negative peer pressure.)*

3. When the boys leave the Seton Hall meeting, they are not instantly committed to attending medical school. Look for the turning points that lead each to choose this path. How must each change his thinking to attain this grand goal of becoming a doctor? *(The decision seems easiest for George, who comes across as the most focused of the three. He leaves the meeting thinking they should apply to the program. His two main motivators appear to be Miss Johnson, who introduces him to the concept of college, and his dentist, who helps him formulate a dream. His biggest obstacle is realizing a good future is available if he seizes the opportunity. Sampson and Rameck are more unsure about college. Both are torn by their neighborhood connections and the allure of street life. For Sampson, the turning point comes when his friends betray him to the police and he spends the summer in a detention center. He realizes there is no loyalty in street life, and he witnesses his mother's anguish when he faces his sentencing. He decides to straighten up. Rameck similarly finds himself in trouble with the law. He experiences the horrors of jail when he spends Thanksgiving there over the near-killing of a crack addict. He vows then to turn his life around. Sampson and Rameck realize they can't have it both ways; they have to leave their old friends behind if they're going to achieve something great.)*

4. Despite their shared experiences and goals, the three young men are distinct individuals. Analyze the personalities of each, indentifying both strengths and weaknesses. What are the core qualities in each that enable him to achieve his goals? *(George comes across as the quietest and most focused of the three. He seems to accept at a younger age the notion that he can achieve a better life if he just keeps working at it. He doesn't fall into the serious kind of trouble the other two encounter. Still, we know he loves to rap, joke around, and play baseball. He enjoys intellectual challenge. He has many friends and a confident manner. He is the rock among the three, never considering the possibility of failure. "Sampson, the man with determination and drive" [p. 178], also struggles with doubts. He was the little kid who was willing to hold the concrete slab, yet he expresses fear of failure more than the other two. He appears to have the most difficulty adjusting to medical school, often feeling confused and out of place. His success can be attributed in part to a*

competitive spirit. He starts trying on the University High entrance test when he sees George working quickly through it: "…he couldn't stand the idea that there might be kids learning things he wouldn't be taught" [p. 63]. He's smart, and he forges on despite the demons of street life that frequently plague him. Rameck is also very intelligent. His principle fault seems to be a lack of self-control, which frequently lands him in trouble, from the time he fights Meatball in the hall to the time he body-slams a fellow dorm resident. He has two brushes with the law and commits a serious offense at Seton Hall, and it is only luck that he doesn't face long-term ramifications. His love of the spotlight suggests a desire to engage people.)

5. What are the keys to the pact's success? Identify points when it might have all fallen apart. In your opinion, would any of the men have become doctors without the pact? *(The pact is successful because of the commitment it inspires in the three boys. For example, Rameck states his interest in attending Howard, but he goes with the other two because of the pact. They push one another to complete the application, and the fact that they're entering the program with a built-in support group seems to interest Carla Dickson during the interviews. The pact's value is probably greatest at college and medical school. Without it, Rameck might have decided to pursue a rap career instead. Sampson's feelings of displacement might have overwhelmed him to the point that he quit school. George seemed to have the best chance of making it on his own, having possessed the vision from a young age. Still, George says, "I think some of my constant pushing and encouraging of Rameck and Sam was based more on my own fear than on my confidence" [p. 27].)*

6. Besides the encouragement the three boys/men provide one another, they also tell stories of other people who positively influenced their lives. Identify some of these people and how they helped shape the personalities and goals of the three doctors. *(Ma shows her belief in Rameck when she won't give him money for fancy new shoes but will give him anything that contributes to a positive future. She offers him emotional support as he deals with his mother's problems. Miss Johnson shows George there's a whole world out there for him—literature, theater, and college. Reggie teaches Sampson how to channel his energies positively and encourages him to dream. Carla Dickson provides a positive and constant presence throughout eight years of higher learning. She scolds them when they're slacking off and encourages them when they're feeling down. Jack warns Sampson about stealing, giving him a glimpse of positive repercussions. The biology teacher gives Rameck a second chance when she could have had him expelled. She knew he had too much promise; expulsion would probably have meant the end of his education. Answers will vary.)*

7. Discuss the mistakes the young men make along the way. How do second chances figure into their success? Can a person be given too many chances? *(When Sampson is involved in robbing drug dealers, he is able to plea as a juvenile and receives a suspended sentence. He comes away from that incident with greater determination to stay out of trouble and seek a better life. Rameck gets a number of second chances as well, first when the biology teacher he sprayed with Silly String stands up for him and then when the mother of the Seton Hall student declines to press assault charges. Leaving school either of these times very likely would have been the end of Rameck's education. Answers will vary regarding when second chances should be given to individuals. Conversation might address justice vs. mercy, feelings of sincere regret, and the failure to learn responsible behavior if a person never suffers consequences.)*

8. One of the lessons the doctors teach is that sometimes you fail before you succeed. Where in the story do we see them learning this lesson? What examples from your own life can you offer that illustrate the value of failure? *(The most prominent example in the book is Sampson's failure to match in a residency that he wants. Without this failure, he might never have landed his dream job. Answers will vary. Students could cite how their low times—like Sampson's or Rameck's times in jail—taught them important lessons about what they wanted from life.)*

9. How do the three young men deal with the ridicule they face for caring about school? Compare the attitudes toward education they encounter with those of your peers. *(Dr. Davis writes, "When I was in school, a good grade could destroy a kid. High marks could open you up to ridicule, to name-calling, to being made an outsider" [p. 65]. When academic success is discouraged, it becomes more difficult for young people to change their situations. All three young men muster the inner courage to succeed, although they acknowledge hiding grades or lying about good academic performance. George at age eight is encouraged by Miss. Johnson and comes to the conclusion, "I guess I really don't care what they think of me" [p. 26]. It helps too that they end up at a high school where kids are more accepting of achievement, and further, that they have the support of one another. Answers will vary.)*

10. In small groups or as a class, make a list of the keys to the three doctors' success. Looking at your list, identify the strategies that are unique to their situation and those that are available to any person striving to achieve. *(Answers will vary. Suggestions: being smart, having good role models, working hard, persevering when things get hard, staying away from drugs, leaving friends who bring them down for those who will support them, the pact, a good college program geared to their needs, families who are willing to make sacrifices for their kids' educations)*

Post-reading Extension Activities

Writing

1. Go to the doctors' Web site, www.threedoctorsfoundation.org. Each of the three doctors' email addresses is listed there. Write a letter to one of the three doctors telling him about your response to his story and any impact it may have had on your life.

2. Choose one of the narrative essays you wrote during your reading of the book. Rewrite the essay in the third person. Use dialogue and add descriptive detail.

3. Write an 18–24 line poem focusing on one of the specific themes of the book: peer pressure, determination, striving to do one's best in school, or friendship.

Music

4. The three doctors tell us they love rap music. Write "The Three Doctors Rap" detailing some aspect of the experiences depicted in the book. Perform your rap for the class.

Social Studies

5. Research the changes that have occurred in Newark, New Jersey since the three doctors grew up there in the 1980s and 1990s. What changes has the city undergone? What effect, if any, are the changes having in the kind of neighborhood in which the doctors grew up? Create a poster based on your findings.

6. The dropout rate in America's inner-city schools is remarkably high. Research your own city or another of your choice, and look for programs geared toward improving academic performance and lowering the dropout rate. Evaluate the effectiveness of one of these programs. Create a brochure to promote the program.

Current Events/Debate

7. In the "Shout-Outs!" at the end of the book, the doctors write, "We owe much of our success to the Pre-Medical/Pre-Dental Plus Program and Access Med, two affirmative-action programs that simply gave us a chance. If we had lived in other states where such programs have come under attack, we probably would not have been afforded the opportunities that helped to make us who we are" (pp. 185–186). Research the history of affirmative-action programs. With a partner, stage a debate on the value and fairness of affirmative action in college admissions.

Speech/Drama

8. Write a scene based on one of the stories in the book for either a movie or stage version of *We Beat the Street*. Perform it for the class.

9. Pretend you are a talk-show host and one of the three doctors is a guest on your show. With a partner, act out this interview for the class.

10. Create a trailer for the movie version of *We Beat the Street*. Convey to the audience the tone and central themes of the story. Provide four or five snippets of what they'll see when they go to the movie.

Art

11. Choose one of the doctors, and create a mural that depicts the path that doctor took to his medical career. Your illustrations for the milestones they hit along the way can be either literal or symbolic.

Assessment for *We Beat the Street*

Assessment is an ongoing process. The following ten items can be completed during study of the book. Once finished, the student and teacher will check the work. Points may be added to indicate the level of understanding.

Name _____ Date _____

Student	Teacher	
_____	_____	1. Working in a small group, write five review questions for your assigned section. Participate in an oral review.
_____	_____	2. Compare two of your completed Supplementary Activities with members of a small group.
_____	_____	3. In a small group, make flash cards of the vocabulary words. Take turns quizzing one another.
_____	_____	4. Complete the Cause/Effect chart on page 25 of this guide.
_____	_____	5. Return to the Initiating Activity where you listed five to ten goals or dreams you have. In a short paragraph, explain whether the book has made those goals feel more easily attainable.
_____	_____	6. Share one Post-reading Extension Activity with the class on an assigned day.
_____	_____	7. Complete a Story Map like the one on page 26 of this guide.
_____	_____	8. Search the Internet for pictures, interviews, and other information about the three doctors. Report any new information to the class.
_____	_____	9. Choose one piece of advice from the book that expresses an idea you agree with or appreciate. Write an essay discussing your understanding of that idea and how you would like to apply it to your own life.
_____	_____	10. Write a bio-poem about one of the three doctors. See page 27 of this guide for directions.

Prediction Chart

What characters have we met so far?	What is the conflict in the story?	What are your predictions?	Why did you make these predictions?

Character Chart

Directions: As you read the book, keep track of the events that happen to each of the authors as well as your impressions of the three as they progress through grade school, high school, college, and medical school.

Sampson	George	Rameck

Characterization

Directions: Write the name of a character from the book in the center rectangle. In each oval, write an adjective that describes the character's personality. Then fill in each dotted rectangle with a detail about the character that illustrates that part of the character's personality.

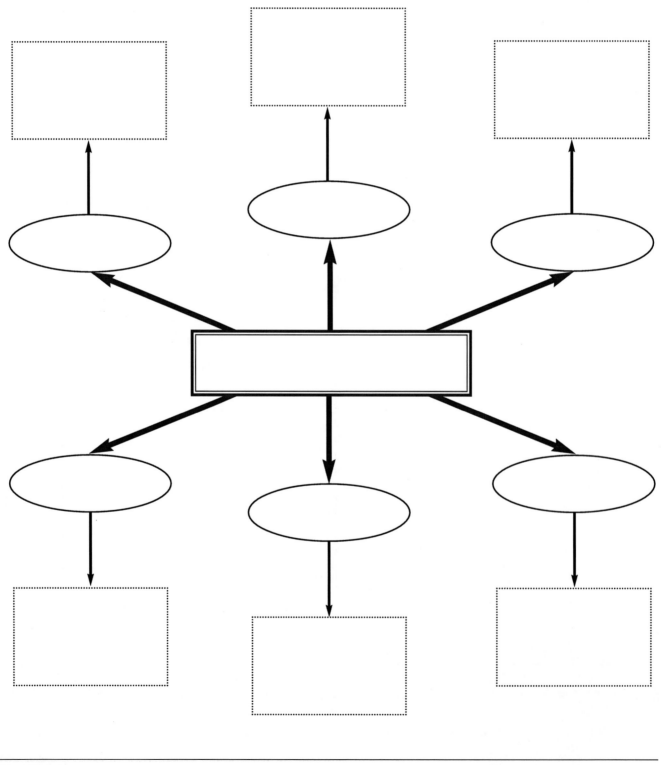

Using Dialogue

Directions: Examine the dialogue between Sampson and Jacquie Johnson, resident coordinator for Newark Beth Israel Hospital. Fill in the chart to evaluate the purpose of the dialogue and whether or not it is effective in advancing the plot.

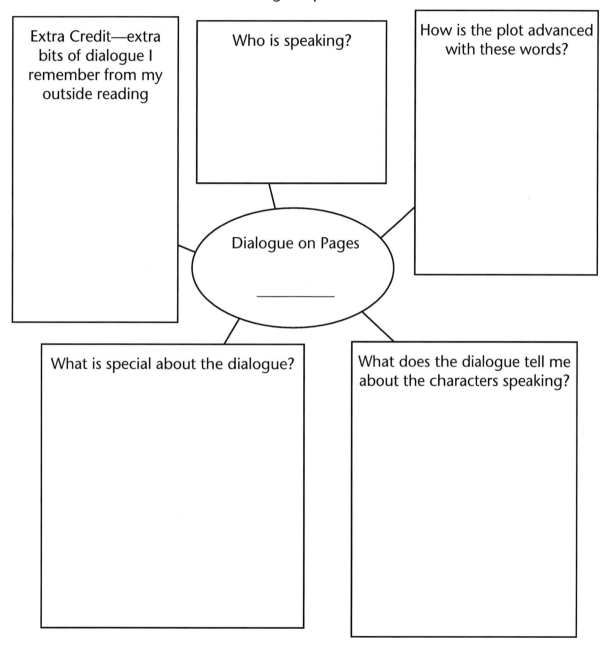

Effects of Reading

Directions: When reading, each part of a book may affect you in a different way. Think about how parts of the book affected you in different ways. Did some parts make you laugh? cry? want to do something to help someone? Below, list one part of the book that touched each of the following parts of the body: your head (made you think), your heart (made you feel), your funny bone (made you laugh), or your feet (spurred you to action).

Your head	Your heart

Your funny bone	Your feet

Cause/Effect

Directions: To plot cause and effect in a book, first list the sequence of events. Then mark causes with a C and effects with an E. Sometimes in a chain of events, one item may be both a cause and an effect. Draw arrows from cause statements to the appropriate effects.

Events in the book	Cause	Effect
1.		
2.		
3.		
4.		
5.		
6.		
7.		
8.		
9.		
10.		

Another way to map cause and effect is to look for an effect and then backtrack to the single or multiple causes.

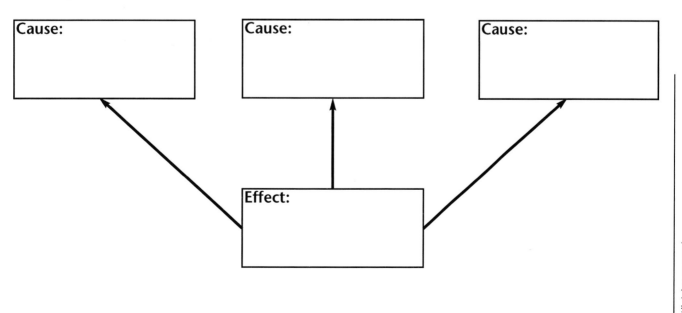

Story Map

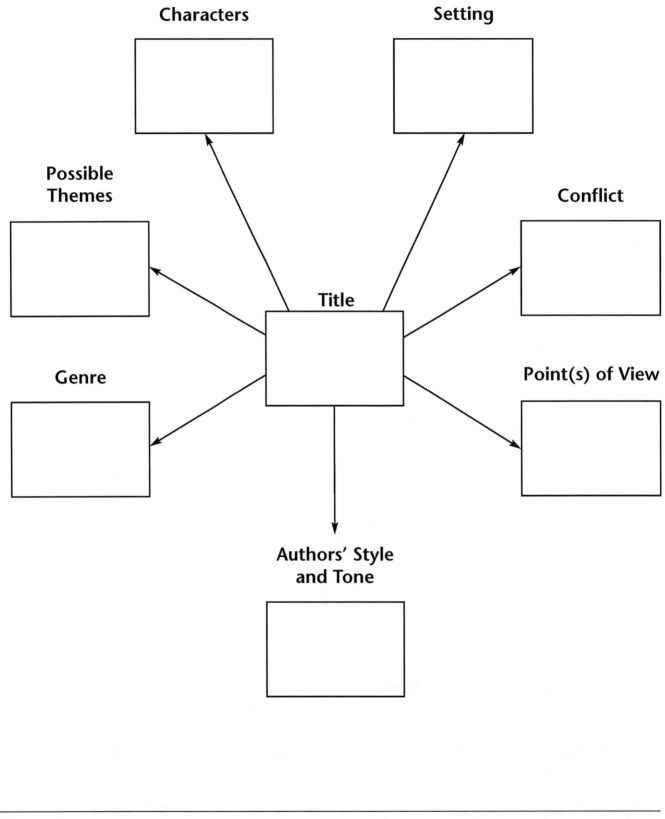

Characters

Setting

Possible
Themes

Conflict

Title

Genre

Point(s) of View

Authors' Style
and Tone

Bio-poem

Directions: Using the format below, write a bio-poem about one of the three doctors. Then write a bio-poem about yourself using the same format. Write a paragraph describing the values and characteristics you share.

—Line 1: First name
—Line 2: three traits of (list three things character loves)
—Line 3: dreams of (list three things character gives)
—Line 4: struggles with (list three things character needs)
—Line 5: fears (list three things character wants)
—Line 6: is good at (list three things character is good at)
—Line 7: regrets (list three things character needs to improve)
—Line 8: has learned (list three people or other characters to whom this character is similar and list a reason behind each character)
—Line 9: exemplifies (list three things the character survives)
—Line 10: "Dr." plus last name

Title _____

1. _____

2. _____

3. _____

4. _____

5. _____

6. _____

7. _____

8. _____

9. _____

10. _____

Linking Novel Units® Lessons to National and State Reading Assessments

During the past several years, an increasing number of students have faced some form of state-mandated competency testing in reading. Many states now administer state-developed assessments to measure the skills and knowledge emphasized in their particular reading curriculum. The discussion questions and post-reading questions in this Novel Units® Teacher Guide make excellent open-ended comprehension questions and may be used throughout the daily lessons as practice activities. The rubric below provides important information for evaluating responses to open-ended comprehension questions. Teachers may also use scoring rubrics provided for their own state's competency test.

Please note: The Novel Units® Student Packet contains optional open-ended questions in a format similar to many national and state reading assessments.

Scoring Rubric for Open-Ended Items

3-Exemplary	Thorough, complete ideas/information Clear organization throughout Logical reasoning/conclusions Thorough understanding of reading task Accurate, complete response
2-Sufficient	Many relevant ideas/pieces of information Clear organization throughout most of response Minor problems in logical reasoning/conclusions General understanding of reading task Generally accurate and complete response
1-Partially Sufficient	Minimally relevant ideas/information Obvious gaps in organization Obvious problems in logical reasoning/conclusions Minimal understanding of reading task Inaccuracies/incomplete response
0-Insufficient	Irrelevant ideas/information No coherent organization Major problems in logical reasoning/conclusions Little or no understanding of reading task Generally inaccurate/incomplete response

Glossary

Introduction–Chapter Four

1. apathy: indifference; lack of interest or concern
2. retrospect: a review of past events; looking back
3. daunting: overwhelming or intimidating
4. swaggered: strutted; paraded; walked with an air of boastfulness
5. hoisted: lifted; heaved
6. intensify: grow stronger or more acute; sharpen
7. loomed: approached, often with a sense of threat or menace; closed in
8. mused: became absorbed in thought; turned over in one's mind
9. sparse: meager; few; scattered
10. debris: the remains of something broken down or destroyed; rubbish
11. asserted: stated or declared positively and often forcefully

Chapters Five–Nine

1. plaintively: expressing sorrow or melancholy; mournfully
2. lanky: ungracefully thin and bony
3. gait: a person's manner of walking
4. inquisitive: prone to asking questions; eager for knowledge; intellectually curious
5. sinews: tendons
6. warily: in a watchful manner; on guard for danger
7. deterrent: something that prevents action; curb; check; preventative
8. regally: befitting or resembling a king; with stateliness; splendidly
9. sauntered: walked at a leisurely pace; strolled
10. lumbered: walked or moved with heavy clumsiness

Chapters Ten–Thirteen

1. malignant: something dangerous or harmful in influence or effect; hateful
2. seethed: excited or emotionally stirred up with anger
3. insubordinate: resisting authority; disobedient
4. entrepreneur: one who organizes, manages, or assumes the risk of a business enterprise
5. incredulously: in a manner unwilling to admit something is true; with disbelief
6. conviction: a strong persuasion or belief; certainty
7. blustery: windy
8. cowering: shrinking away from something menacing
9. bravado: blustering, swaggering conduct; a pretense of bravery
10. bristled: took on an aggressive, defensive attitude

Chapters Fourteen–Seventeen

1. exulted: felt or expressed joy or triumph; rejoiced
2. unfazed: undisturbed; undaunted
3. loping: walking with an easy, bounding gate
4. admonished: expressed warning or disapproval of, usually in a gently or solicitous manner
5. brash: bold; audacious
6. remediation: the act or process of remedying; correction
7. affirmation: a positive assertion; the act of affirming; validation

8. pulmonary: of, relating to, or occurring in the lungs
9. antagonize: to incur or invoke the hostility of
10. dissipated: slowly broken up or scattered

Chapters Eighteen–Conclusion

1. tumultuous: marked by overwhelming turbulence or upheaval; stormy
2. acclimated: adapted to a new climate, environment, or situation
3. livid: very angry; enraged
4. genially: with sympathy or friendliness
5. limbo: a state of transition or uncertainty; in flux
6. palatable: agreeable to taste; agreeable to the mind

Notes

Notes